靜思精舍惜物造福的智慧故事❺

智慧
本草飲的故事

總策劃 / 靜思書軒

The Wisdom of Cherishing and Sowing Blessings
at the Jing Si Abode (5)
Wisdom: The Story of the Jing Si Herbal Tea

小慧走出房間擔心的問：「阿公還好嗎？」

爸爸說：「阿公被送進花蓮慈濟醫院時，已經意識不清了，有發高燒、呼吸困難的症狀，情況很緊急。幸好他在重症病房受到細心照顧，漸漸恢復了。」

Xiao-Hui asked worriedly as she came out of the room, "Is grandpa all right?"

Xiao-Hui's father said, "Grandpa was already unconscious when he was sent to Hualien Tzu Chi Hospital, with a high fever and trouble breathing. It's a good thing he received good care at the hospital, and he's getting better."

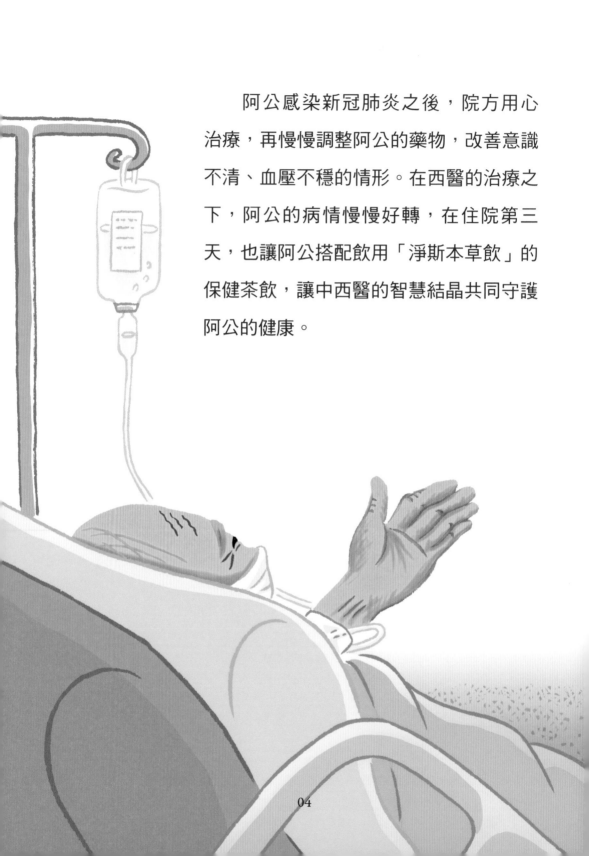

阿公感染新冠肺炎之後，院方用心治療，再慢慢調整阿公的藥物，改善意識不清、血壓不穩的情形。在西醫的治療之下，阿公的病情慢慢好轉，在住院第三天，也讓阿公搭配飲用「淨斯本草飲」的保健茶飲，讓中西醫的智慧結晶共同守護阿公的健康。

The hospital took good care of grandpa after he caught COVID-19, gradually treating problems such as grandpa losing consciousness and his unstable blood pressure. He began to recover after getting treatment from western medicine, and starting from the third day, grandpa was also given Jing Si Herbal Tea, a healthy tea drink. The combined wisdom of western and Chinese medicine helped grandpa regain his health.

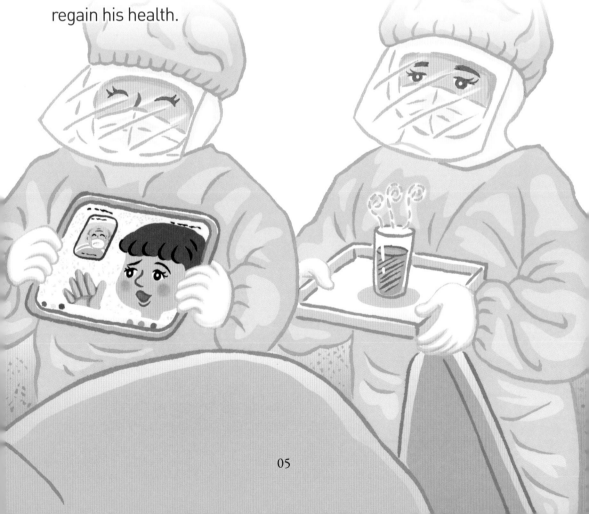

　　小慧說：「阿公，歡迎回家！看到阿公完全好了，真是阿彌陀佛！」

　　阿公說：「呵呵，小慧也會阿彌陀佛。我住院的時候，除了西藥，也有喝『淨斯本草飲』來調養身心健康，你們也可以喝喔！」

Xiao-Hui exclaimed, "Grandpa, you're home! Thank the Buddha you're all right!"

Grandpa replied, "Ha ha! Xiao-Hui also knows to thank the Buddha, I see. When I was in the hospital, I didn't just take western medicine, I also drank Jing Si Herbal Tea as I recovered my health. You should all try it too!"

小慧問：「爸爸，『淨斯本草飲』是怎麼發明的？」

爸爸說：「這是證嚴上人想到以前去探病、掃墓或參加喪禮回來後，大人會用煮過的艾草和抹草（魚針草）水洗一洗，有辟邪和抗菌的功效。」小慧說：「是端午節掛在門上的艾草！」

「於是，請花蓮慈濟醫院林欣榮院長、專長中醫的何宗融副院長以及負責研究的黃志揚副院長團隊和慈濟基金會的林碧玉副總團隊把這幾種藥草帶回去研究，看看能不能研發對大家有幫助的保健食品，提升對抗新冠病毒的抵抗力。」

Xiao-Hui asked, "Daddy, how was Jing Si Herbal Tea made?

Xiao-Hui's father replied, "Dharma Master Cheng Yen remembered that, in the past, whenever she visited someone who was sick, went tomb sweeping, or attended a funeral, the adults in her family would boil argyi (Chinese mugwort) and Kalabhangra (mo cao or Anisomeles indica) plant in water and bathe her with that water. They said this would help fight germs and ward off bad spirits."

Xiao-Hui asked, "Oh, you mean the Chinese mugwort we hang on our door during the Dragon Boat Festival?"

"That's the one," Xiao-Hui's father replied, "So the Dharma Master asked the Superintendent Dr. Shinn-Zong Lin, the Vice Superintendent and Chinese medicine expert Dr. Tsung-Jung Ho, and the Vice Superintendent Dr. Chih-Yang Huang of Hualien Tzu Chi Hospital, as well as Vice President Pi-Yu Lin of the Tzu Chi Foundation to bring these herbs back to the hospital and study them. She asked them to see if they could create something that would help people fight the COVID-19 virus."

爸爸說：「集結了中醫和西醫團隊，整合臺灣本土的中草藥，開發中藥包進行實驗，2020年底終於研發出由艾葉、魚針草、麥冬、魚腥草、桔梗、甘草、紫蘇葉、菊花等八種本土中草藥製成的『淨斯本草飲』。」
小慧說：「爸爸，走！我們去聽林欣榮院長演講。」

Xiao-Hui's father continued, "With the leadership of Superintendent Lin, a team of eastern and western medicine experts gathered together all the Chinese medicine herbs grown in Taiwan to do experiments. In late 2020, they developed the Jing Si Herbal Tea, made from eight different herbs: argyi leaf, Kalabhangra, Ophiopogonis radix, dokudami, balloon flower, glycyrrhizae radix, perilla, and chrysanthemi flos."
Xiao-Hui exclaimed, "Come on, dad! Let's go to the Jing Si Abode to hear Superintendent Shinn-Zong Lin talk about the Jing Si Herbal Tea!"

【桔梗】

【艾葉】

【紫蘇葉】

【甘草】

【麥冬】

【魚針草】

【菊花】

【魚腥草】

11

林院長說：「謝謝大家來聽我說『淨斯本草飲』的故事。2020年5月新冠肺炎病毒席捲臺灣。上人說這個時代就是『大哉教育』，是全球受教育的機會，好好地接受這一波天地給予人類的教育。花蓮慈濟醫院研發團隊，接受上人的指示，進行艾草和抹草的研究。」

Superintendent Lin said, "Thank you all for coming to hear me speak about the Jing Si Herbal Tea. In May 2020, the COVID-19 epidemic swept across Taiwan. Dharma Master Cheng Yen said this was an opportunity for a 'great lesson of our times,' in which the whole world could learn something from nature. So the research team at Hualien Tzu Chi Hospital also followed the Dharma Master's instructions and started researching argyi (Chinese mugwort) and Kalabhangra (mo cao or Anisomeles indica)."

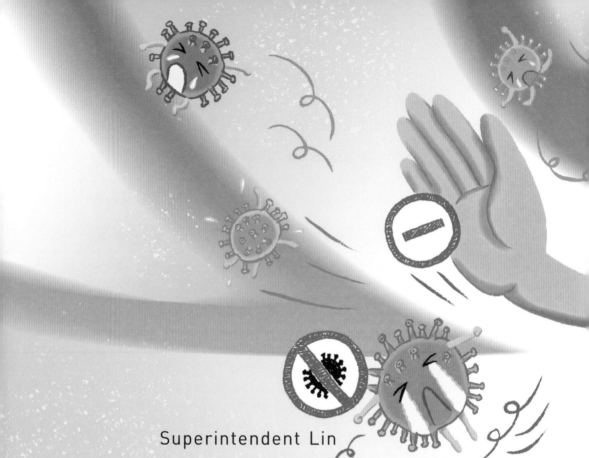

Superintendent Lin continued, "In Chinese medicine, it is important to strengthen both the inside and the outside of the body. Take the yin-yang symbol as an example, balance between the yin and yang is needed for a healthy body. When there is not enough positive energy in the body, then the yang must be boosted. In Chinese medicine, the eight herbs in the Jing Si Herbal Tea help 'improve the body's strength and ward off negative factors.' Here, 'negative factors' means plagues, cancer, and aging."

　　林院長又說：「中醫重視身體內外的調和來強健身心，以太極圖為例，陰陽平衡才是身體健康的狀態。當人體的正氣不足，就需要用『陽』提升。而『淨斯本草飲』這八種藥材組合在一起，發揮的正是中醫所說的『扶正祛邪』，『邪』指的是瘟疫、癌症和老化。」

「短短兩個月，研發團隊就接到藥草可以收成的消息，原來精舍的師父們早在我們討論階段時就開始種植藥草，還有志工們提供種子，真的很感恩大家！」

　　"The research team received word that the herbs were ready for harvest in just two short months! It turned out that Dharma Masters at the Jing Si Abode already started planting the herbs when they heard us discussing them. Some volunteers even donated the seeds for free. We were truly grateful!"

「藥草除了由淨斯藥草園種植外，也從全臺各地買藥草，並由『靜思人文』負責大量生產。」

"Aside from the herbs grown at the Jing Si Abode, we also bought many herbs from all over Taiwan. The tea itself was produced by 'Jing Si Culture.' "

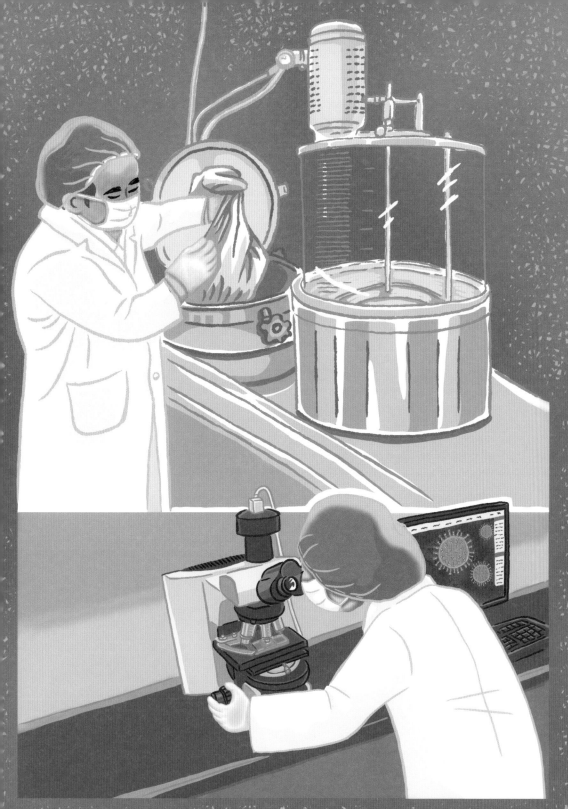

林院長說：「上人不僅提倡中西醫合療，也重視中草藥的研究。『淨斯本草飲』這項保健飲品在醫學和醫藥、科技相關領域擁有多項成就以及影響力，上人還獲頒美國國家發明家科學院院士認證。」

　　Superintendent Lin said, "Dharma Master Cheng Yen advocates for integrative approaches of western and Chinese medicine, and she also believes that researching Chinese medicinal herbs is very important. We have made several accomplishments in medical sciences in the research and development of the Jing Si Herbal Tea, and it's become quite influential. The Dharma Master was even accepted as a Fellow of the National Academy of Inventors in the United States!"

　　矇矓中，小慧聽到林院長的介紹：

　　「花蓮慈濟醫院中西醫的整合，不只是在研究上合作，從急診、門診、加護病房到安寧病房與長照，都提供民眾中西醫會診治療的選擇。其中，上人命名的中醫病房『自在居』，以中西醫雙主治醫師為訴求，提供醫療照護。」

Xiao-Hui heard, as if in a dream, Superintendent Lin introducing the hospital, "At Hualien Tzu Chi Hospital, western and Chinese medicine are integrated not just in research, but also in emergency care, outpatient care, the ICU, and even palliative and long-term care. We offer patients the option of receiving both Chinese and western medicine consultations. Dharma Master Cheng Yen also named the Chinese medicine ward 'Zizai Ward' in Chinese, which means 'to live at ease.' Here, Chinese medicine and western medicine doctors work together to provide care to patients."

林院長看到小慧，說：「難得有小朋友來參加，小妹妹，你想知道什麼？」

　　小慧說：「請問有沒有比較好喝的淨斯本草飲？」引來一陣笑聲。

　　林院長說：「淨斯本草飲有茶包、濃縮液兩種型態，可依自己的需求沖調，很好入口。」

Superintendent Lin noticed Xiao-Hui in the audience, and said, "We don't see kids at these speeches very often. Is there something you would like to ask?"

Xiao-Hui asked, "Is there a type of Jing Si Herbal Tea that tastes nicer?" Many people in the audience chuckled.

Superintendent Lin replied, "The Jing Si Herbal Tea comes in tea bag and concentrate forms. You can choose how you want to make it. It's quite delicious!"

小慧說：「上人是臺灣之光！」

爸爸說：「上人支持中西醫合療，花蓮慈濟醫院也致力於此。希望他們透過淨斯本草系列保健飲品的研究，中西醫的通力合作，幫助更多人。」

小慧說：「以後我也要善用我的智慧，造福人群！」

Xiao-Hui said, "Dharma Master Cheng Yen really is the Pride of Taiwan!"

Xiao-Hui's father said, "The Dharma Master supports an integrative approach of Chinese and western medicine, so that's what the doctors at Hualien Tzu Chi Hospital are doing. I hope they'll be able to help more people by studying health drinks like the Jing Si Herbal Tea and by working together."

Xiao-Hui declared, "When I grow up, I'm also going to use my wisdom to help as many people as I can!"

一起動手做做看
Let's try making it!

看完「淨斯本草飲」的故事，和大人一起來做淨斯本草藥膳湯和淨斯本草茶凍，好玩、好吃又健康！

After learning about the story of the Jing Si Herbal Tea, let's try making some Jing Si Herbal Soup and Jing Si Herbal Jelly with an adult!

健康美味本草飲藥膳湯食譜
Recipe for Jing Si Herbal Soup

材料 Ingredients

淨斯本草飲茶包	2 包	2 tea bags of Jing Si Herbal Tea
高麗菜	1/4 顆	1/4 head of cabbage
油炸過的乾豆皮	45 克	45g of deep-fried dried tofu skins
金針菇	150 克	150g of enoki mushrooms
雪白菇 50 克		50g of white beech mushrooms
鴻喜菇 50 克		50g of beech mushrooms
鹽 適量		Salt to taste
生薑片 5 片約 20 克		5 slices of raw ginger, approximately 20g

❶ 煮一鍋水，放入「淨斯本草飲」茶包，待水滾，轉小火，熬煮5 分鐘後，撈出茶包。

Add water to a pot, and then add the Jing Si Herbal Tea bags. Boil the water, turn the heat to low, and simmer for 5 minutes. Then remove the tea bags.

❷ 「淨斯本草飲」的茶湯性涼，先下薑片熬煮 1 分鐘，再放耐煮的菇類，高麗菜。待高麗菜煮到半軟時，放入乾豆皮，為湯頭的油脂來源。

The Jing Si Herbal Tea is considered cool-natured in Chinese medicine, therefore first add the sliced ginger and boil for 1 minute, before adding the beech mushrooms, white beech mushrooms, and cabbage. When the cabbage is partially cooked, add the dried tofu skins, which will add fat to the soup.

鹽

❸ 待豆皮煮軟後，放入金針菇，等到湯頭煮滾，放適量的鹽提味，一道鮮美的藥膳湯即大功告成。

After the tofu skins soften, add the enoki mushrooms and bring to a boil. Add salt to taste. The Jing Si Herbal Soup is complete.

1.「淨斯本草飲」茶包熬煮 5 分鐘即可撈起，熬煮時間短，保留茶湯清甜的部分作為藥膳湯基底。

2. 青菜的選擇上，以味道樸實的高麗菜為首選，不僅增加湯頭的鮮甜，也不會搶了藥膳的味道。

3. 坊間多數藥膳湯大多會放枸杞，可以增添湯頭的風味，但是淨斯本草藥膳湯的本草飲性質清泄，為避免藥性衝突，不建議加性質偏補的枸杞。

1. The Jing Si Herbal Tea bag should be removed after 5 minutes. This is because a shorter boiling time will help preserve the natural sweetness of the tea and improve the flavor as a base for the soup.

2. Cabbage is the best choice of vegetable due to its mild taste. It adds sweetness to the soup while not covering the flavors of the herbs.

3. Many herbal soup recipes include goji berries, which can improve the flavor. However, the Jing Si Herbal Tea's herbs are considered cool-natured in Chinese medicine, and goji berries are hot-natured, so they may conflict with the existing herbs. Therefore, adding goji berries is not recommended.

清爽可口本草飲茶凍食譜
Recipe for Jing Si Herbal Jelly

材料 Ingredients

淨斯本草飲茶包	2 包	2 tea bags of Jing Si Herbal Tea
黑糖	10 克	10g of brown sugar
吉利 T 粉	15 克	15g of agar-agar powder

＊小注釋：食譜中的吉利 T 是天然植物海藻萃取的植物性膠質，與一般所知的吉利丁是動物的皮或骨提煉出來的膠質，不太一樣喔！

＊ Note : The agar-agar in the recipe is made from natural seaweed, while gelatin is extracted from animal skins or bones. They are not the same!

❶ 盛 一 鍋 600c.c. 的 水，放入煮過的「淨斯本草飲」茶包，待水滾轉小火煮 10 分鐘後，撈出茶包，茶湯熄火備用。

Add 600c.c. of water to a pot, and then add the Jing Si Herbal Tea bags that have already been boiled in the previous recipe. Bring the water to a boil, turn the heat to low, and simmer for 10 minutes. Then remove the tea bags and turn off the heat.

❷ 取另一湯鍋，盛入100c.c. 的水煮滾，轉小火；把吉利T和黑糖拌勻，倒入煮開的熱水中快速攪散，攪拌到色澤呈現透亮凍狀的程度。

黑糖 ＋ 吉利T

拌勻
↓
快速攪拌

Add 100c.c. of water to another pot and bring to a boil, and then turn the heat to low. Mix the agar-agar and brown sugar, and then add them to the boiled water and stir vigorously until the mixture is translucent.

❸ 再把茶湯倒入湯鍋中，
一邊倒一邊攪，充分混
合。

Add the hot tea to the
mixture, stirring as you
pour, until it is thoroughly
mixed.

放涼

❹ 趁熱倒入模具，靜置
放涼後結成茶凍即
成。茶凍上撒一些花
生碎或搭配鮮奶、蜂
蜜、黑糖蜜，滋味很
不錯！

Add the mixture to molds while it is hot. Let rest to cool, and
the jelly is complete. The flavor of the jelly can be improved by
sprinkling peanuts on top or adding milk, honey, or molasses.

注意事項 Important Note

1. 淨斯本草茶凍的發想來自龜苓膏，用已煮過的「淨斯本草飲」茶包小火熬煮 10 分鐘，熬煮時間較久，才能把較苦的藥味煮出來。

2. 每家吉利 T 的廠牌不同，與水混合的比例不一樣，所以要參考購買的吉利 T 的營養標示及作法，抓出水與吉利 T 的比例，才能做出完美的茶凍。

1. The recipe for the Jing Si Herbal Jelly was based on guilinggao. By boiling previously-boiled tea bags for 10 minutes, the longer boiling time will bring out the bitterness of the herbs.

2. The agar-agar produced by different companies will require different amounts of water. Please refer to the instructions specific to the agar-agar you have bought to find the right ratio of water to agar-agar.

草藥保健其來有自

我們對中醫的草藥治病、保健並不陌生，其實，歐洲也有草藥治病的醫療文化。

《藥物論》由希臘醫生迪奧斯科里德斯在西元 50 至 70 年間完成，記錄 600 多種藥用植物的外觀、生長地、採集方式、藥劑調製及治療效果，並提出以鴉片作為外科麻醉藥的觀點。

英國的外科醫生約翰・傑勒德在 1597 年出版《草本志》。書裡記載一些民間的藥用知識，例如讓黃疸病人洗過澡後服用開黃花的茼蒿，可以恢復正常的膚色。

《草藥實證藥典》是由德國草藥委員會和德國醫學研究部門幾十年研究的結果，書裡詳細記錄全球 254 種已獲證實的草藥的使用方法和作用。自 1994 年出版後，它成為世界上最權威的草藥專書。

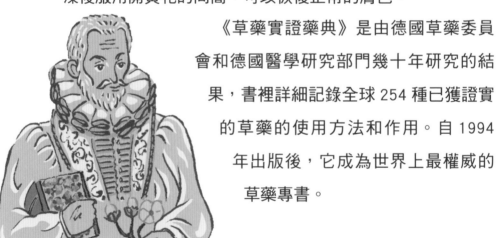

Origins of Using Chinese Herbs for Health

While you may be familiar with the usage of herbs in Chinese medicine, but you may be interested to know that there is also a culture of treating sicknesses with herbs in Europe.

Between 50 to 70 CE, the Greek physician Pedanius Dioscorides wrote *De materia medica*, a record of over 600 herbal plants and their appearances, the places they grow, the methods to collect them, instructions for using them in medicines, and their effects. He also proposed using opium as an anesthetic for surgery.

The British physician John Gerard published *Herball, or Generall Historie of Plantes*, in 1597. The book records folk knowledge on medicine, such as using chrysanthemum with yellow flowers on jaundice patients after bathing to return their skin to the normal color.

In Germany, the Commission E and the Federal Institute for Drugs and Medical Devices published *The Complete German Commission E* after decades of research. The book has detailed records of the uses and effects of 254 herbs from around the world that have been proven to work. Since its publication in 1994, it has become the authoritative source for herbal medicines.

靜思語：智慧

有智慧的人能捨，能「捨」就能「得」，
得到無限的快樂。

A wise person is able to let go.
To let go is actually to receive,
to receive boundless happiness.

《中英對照靜思語 2》｜《小學生 365 靜思語》

「慈心」不能缺乏親善的態度，
「智慧」不能缺乏謙虛的涵養。

To be kind and loving, we must be friendly and amiable.
To be wise, we must be humble.

《中英對照靜思小語 1》｜《小學生 365 靜思語》

透過煩惱轉成智慧，這個煩惱才有意義。

When we become wiser due to an affliction,
then that affliction is meaningful.

《中英對照靜思小語 3》｜《小學生 365 靜思語》

用智慧探討人生真義，用毅力安排人生時間。

Contemplate the meaning of life with wisdom.
Organize the time we are given with resolve.

《中英對照靜思語1》|《小學生365靜思語》

有愛心就有福氣、毅力，才有智慧。

The love in one's heart will bring forth blessings,
perseverance and finally wisdom.

《靜思語第三集》|《小學生365靜思語》

關於本草飲

給老師和家長們更多關於本草飲的資訊。

抹草豐收，常住二眾和志工整理採收回來的抹草，仔細用剪刀將抹草的嫩葉及嫩莖剪下、枝葉分離。
（攝影者：楊采蓉）

2022 年醫療科技展在臺北南港展覽館展出，花蓮慈濟醫學中心也加入參展行列。

　　由慈濟醫學中心中西醫團隊及教授群與五位博士、靜思團隊共同研發，本草飲是體現匯聚眾善，草本護身的結晶。嚴選臺灣本土八種草本成份：麥冬、魚腥草、桔梗、魚針草、甘草、艾葉、紫蘇葉、菊花。從原料的運輸，到清洗、烘乾、磨粉、加工、包裝等，皆獨立生產製作，堅持不含防腐劑、不添加人工香料、色素，全素食，帶給大眾最純淨的來源。

　　找時間走訪一趟「靜思書軒」門市，了解本草飲系列產品，聰明守護健康！

靜思人文
JING SI CULTURE

靜思精舍惜物造福的智慧故事 5

智慧：本草飲的故事

總 策 劃 / 靜思書軒
編 審 / 釋德晗、花蓮慈濟醫學中心中西醫團隊
照片提供 / 慈濟基金會文史處
故 事 / 羅文翠
插 圖 / 王佩娟
美術設計 / 羅吟軒
英 譯 / Linguitronics Co., Ltd. 萬象翻譯（股）公司（故事及主題延伸）

總 編 輯 / 李復民
副總編輯 / 鄧懿貞
特約主編 / 陳佳聖
封面設計 / Javick 工作室
專案企劃 / 蔡孟庭、盤惟心

讀書共和國出版集團 業務平台
總經理 / 李雪麗　　　　　副總經理 / 李復民
海外業務總監 / 張鑫峰　　特販業務總監 / 陳綺瑩
零售資深經理 / 郭文弘　　專案企劃總監 / 蔡孟庭
印務協理 / 江域平　　　　印務主任 / 李孟儒

出 版 / 發光體文化 / 遠足文化事業股份有限公司
發 行 / 遠足文化事業股份有限公司（讀書共和國出版集團）
地 址 / 231 新北市新店區民權路 108 之 2 號 9 樓
電 話 /（02）2218-1417　傳真 /（02）8667-1065
電子信箱 / service@bookrep.com.tw
網 址 / www.bookrep.com.tw
郵撥帳號 / 19504465 遠足文化事業股份有限公司

法律顧問 / 華洋法律事務所 蘇文生律師
印 製 / 凱林彩印股份有限公司

慈濟人文出版社
地 址 / 臺北市忠孝東路三段二一七巷七弄十九號一樓
電 話 /（02）2898-9888
傳 真 /（02）2898-9889
網 址 / www.jingsi.org

2024 年 5 月 2 日初版一刷　　　定價 / 320 元
ISBN / 978-626-98109-5-6（精裝）　書號 / 2IGN1009

國家圖書館出版品預行編目 (CIP) 資料

靜思精舍惜物造福的智慧故事 . 5, 智慧：本草飲的故事 =
The wisdom of cherishing and sowing blessings at the
Jing Si Abode. 5, wisdom : the story of herbal tea / 陳佳
聖故事 . -- 初版 . -- 新北市：遠足文化事業股份有限公司發
光體文化，遠足文化事業股份有限公司，2024.04
　面；　公分
中英對照
ISBN 978-626-98109-5-6(精裝)

224.515　　　　　　　　　　　　113003669